Summer

Spring

Seasons

Written by Emily Bone

Illustrated by Maribel Lechuga

Designed by Anna Gould
and Zoe Wray

Fall

Winter

Seasons consultant: Zoë Simmons
Reading consultant: Alison Kelly

It's spring. There is lots of rain followed by warm sunshine. This makes flowers grow.

Tulip

Daffodil

Crocus

3

Some trees and bushes grow
flowers too. Birds eat the flowers.

Cedar waxwing

Forsythia

House
finch

Red
maple

Apple blossom

Northern cardinal

5

Birds build nests in the spring.

Swans pile up twigs and reeds to make a nest at the side of a river.

The mother swan lays eggs. She sits on them to keep them warm.

Babies hatch out of the eggs.

Baby swans are
called cygnets.

The cygnets follow
their parents into
the river.

Many animals have babies.

Deer have babies called fawns.

Wolf babies are called pups.
They're born in underground dens.

Frogs lay hundreds of eggs.

Frog eggs are
called frogspawn.

Tadpoles grow
inside the eggs.

They hatch out and grow into frogs.

9

In summer, it becomes much warmer.
Summer flowers grow.

Bees, butterflies and other
bugs feed from the flowers.

Marjoram

Fennel

Ox-eye daisy

Bumble bee

Hoverfly

Monarch
butterfly

Black-eyed Susan

Chafer
beetle

Butterflies lay eggs on plants in the summer.

Small white butterfly

Egg

A caterpillar hatches out of the egg. It eats the leaves.

Caterpillar

Birds catch caterpillars.

Blue tits

They feed the caterpillars
to their chicks.

Trees grow leaves and the grass grows long in summer.

Animals eat the trees and grass.

Sheep

Rabbits

Harvest mice live
in long grass.

They weave the grass
into round nests.

Summer nights are warm.
Some creatures are awake.

Hawkmoths feed
from flowers.

Other moths look
for partners.

Silk moths

Giant leopard moth

Agave flowers only open at night.
Bats feed from them.

Agave
flower

Mexican
long-nosed bats

Badgers hunt for worms and
beetles to eat.

As summer changes to fall, fruits
and nuts become ready to eat.

Apple

Blackberry

Rose hips
grow from
rose flowers.

Acorns grow
on oak trees.

Some drop to the
ground. Animals
eat them.

Wild boar

Some animals collect food that they will eat during the winter.

Acorn woodpeckers make holes in trees to store nuts.

Squirrels bury nuts under the ground.

Black bears eat fruits and nuts during the fall. They won't need to eat for the whole of winter.

Mountain ash berries

The weather starts to cool down. The leaves on trees turn red, orange, yellow and brown.

The wind blows. Leaves flutter off the trees.

Maple leaf

Ash leaf

They settle on
the ground.

23

It gets colder later in the fall.

Swallows fly away
to places that have
warmer weather.

They gather in big
groups before they go.

Other animals try to stay warm.

Hedgehogs make warm nests in leaves.
They sleep in the nests all winter.

Peacock butterflies find warm places
such as sheds to rest.

It gets very, very cold in the winter. Plants die and many trees have no leaves.

White tailed deer

Sometimes it snows. Snow settles on the cold ground.

There isn't much for animals to eat. Some birds eat food that they collected during the fall.

Blue jay

Peanut

Animals have to keep warm.

Birds fluff out their feathers and huddle together.

Bluebirds

Mice dig tunnels under the snow where it's warmer.

Owls hunt for mice hiding under the snow. A great gray owl hears a mouse moving.

It swoops down into the snow.

It uses its sharp claws to grab the mouse.

Some animals can find food
even when it's very cold.

Bison use their noses to push
snow out of the way. They eat
the grass underneath.

Holly trees grow berries in late fall.
Birds eat them during winter.

Thrush

Holly

Deer eat fruit, nuts and grass during
summer. In winter, they eat twigs
and moss instead.

Roe deer

31

At the end of winter, plants begin
to grow again. Snowdrops are
one of the first flowers to grow.

Snowdrops

Digital retouching by John Russell